Clean  and Tidy

First published in 2011
by Wayland

Text copyright © Claire Llewellyn
Photograph copyright © Wayland
with the exception of the graphics on p3, 6 and 18 all © Istock

Wayland
338 Euston Road
London NW1 3BH

Wayland Australia
Level 17/207 Kent Street
Sydney, NSW 2000

The rights of Claire Llewellyn to be identified as the Author of this Work have been
asserted by her in accordance with the Copyright, Designs and Patents Act, 1988.

Series Editor: Louise John
Editor: Katie Powell
Design: D.R.ink
Photographer: Andy Crawford
Consultant: Shirley Bickler

A CIP catalogue record for this book is available from the British Library.

ISBN 9780750263818

Printed in China

Wayland is a division of Hachette Children's Books,
an Hachette UK Company

www.hachette.co.uk

With thanks to Carys and Rhian Morris

Every effort has been made to clear copyright. Should there be
any inadvertent omission, please apply to the
publisher for rectification.

Contents

In the morning

In the morning I get up.

I have to get ready to go to school.
I have to look clean and tidy.

My hands and face

First I wash my hands and face.

I fill the basin,
I wet my face cloth
and I **wash, wash, wash!**

Face cloth

Tap

Basin

Soap

My teeth

Then I clean my teeth.

Mum says:
Brushing your teeth keeps germs away.

I put some toothpaste on my toothbrush and I **brush, brush, brush!**

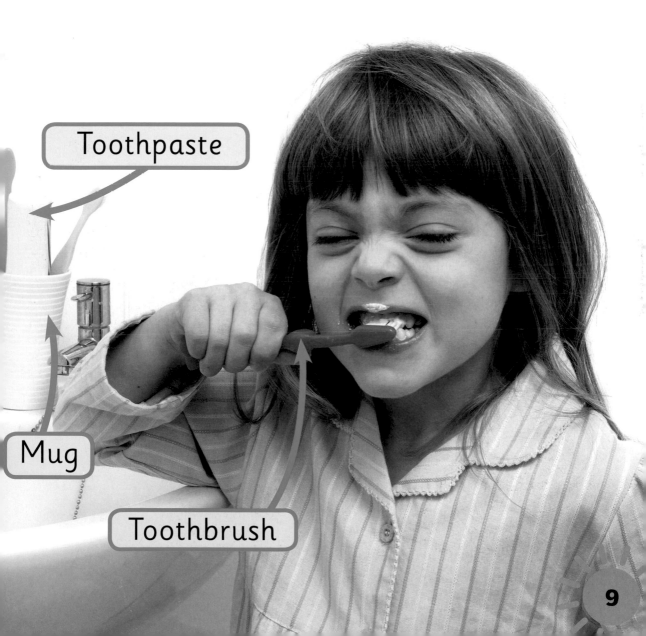

Toothpaste

Mug

Toothbrush

Clean clothes

Then I put on my clean clothes.
I tuck in my T-shirt and
I pull up my socks.

My shoes are dirty,
so Mum gives them a rub.
Rub, rub, rub!

Mum says:
Put your dirty
clothes in the wash.

My hair

Last of all Mum brushes my hair.
Brush, brush, brush!

Mirror

Hairbrush

Now I am clean and tidy.
I am ready for school!

Germs and skin

I am busy all day long.
I work, I run and I play.

I get hot and sticky and dirty.

Mum says:
Dirty hands have lots of germs on them.

In the  **bath**

At night I have a bath.
I wash my skin with soap.

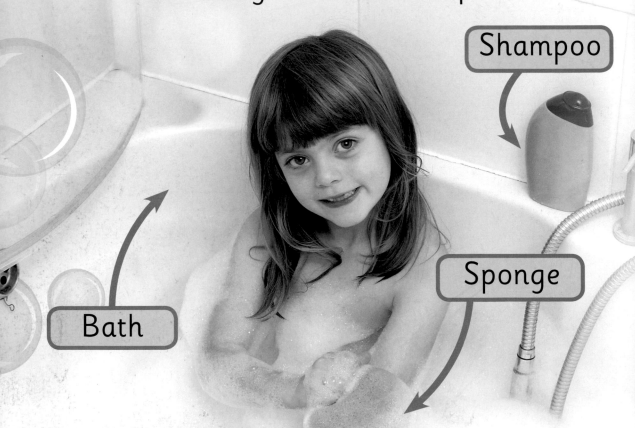

Shampoo

Sponge

Bath

16

Mum says:
Washing gets rid of germs.
It makes you smell sweet!

Mum washes my hair.
Rub, rub, rub!

Shower

My nails

Mum cuts my nails on a Sunday.
Snip, snip, snip!

Scissors

If my nails are dirty,
I scrub them with a brush.
Scrub, scrub, scrub!

Mum says:
Dirty nails
have germs.

Nail brush

I get dirty!

Some days I get very dirty.

So, I **wash, wash, wash.**
I **rub, rub, rub.**
I **scrub, scrub, scrub.**
I **brush, brush, brush,**
and I am clean and tidy again!

Clean and tidy!

What do you use
to tidy your hair?

What do you use to
look after your nails?

What do you use to
wash your face?

What do you use to
clean your teeth?

Shampoo

Nail
scissors

Hairbrush

22

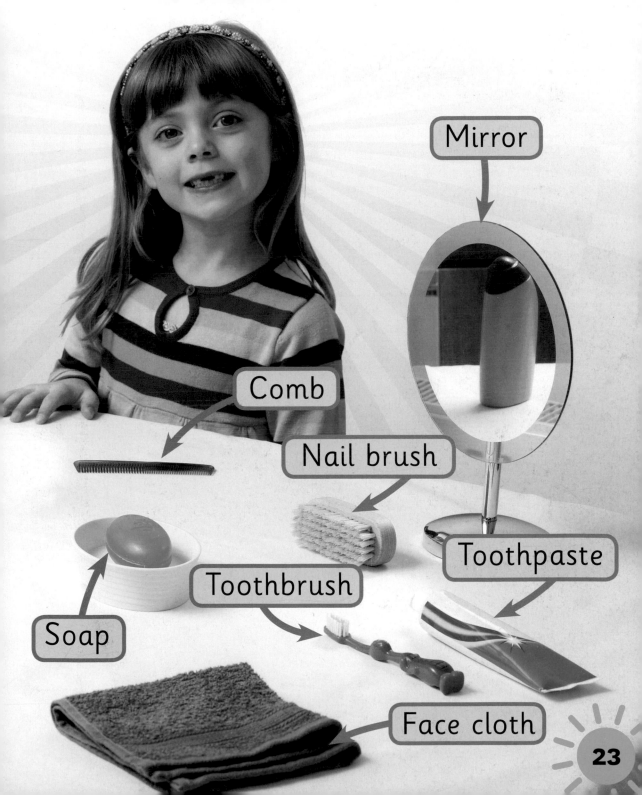

Mirror

Comb

Nail brush

Toothpaste

Soap

Toothbrush

Face cloth

23

START READING is a series of highly enjoyable books for beginner readers. **The books have been carefully graded to match the Book Bands widely used in schools.** This enables readers to be sure they choose books that match their own reading ability.

Look out for the Band colour on the book in our Start Reading logo.

The Bands are:

Pink Band 1A & 1B

Red Band 2

Yellow Band 3

Blue Band 4

Green Band 5

Orange Band 6

Turquoise Band 7

Purple Band 8

Gold Band 9

START READING books can be read independently or shared with an adult. They promote the enjoyment of reading through satisfying stories and non-fiction narratives, which are supported by fun illustrations and photographs.

Claire Llewellyn has written many books for children. Some of them are about real things like animals and the Moon, others are storybooks. Claire has two children, but they are getting too big for her books now. She hopes you will enjoy reading them instead!